A Tree of My Own

TALKING CUB
Published by Speaking Tiger Books LLP
125A, Ground Floor, Shahpur Jat
New Delhi 110049

First published in paperback in Talking Cub by Speaking Tiger Books in 2022
Text copyright © Ruskin Bond 2022
Illustrations copyright © Barkha Lohia 2022

ISBN: 978-93-5447-398-2
eISBN: 978-93-5447-399-9

10 9 8 7 6 5 4 3 2 1

Printed at

No part of this publication may be reproduced, transmitted, or stored in a retrieval system, in any form or by any means, electronic, mechanical, photocopying, recording or otherwise, without the prior permission of the publisher.

This book is sold subject to the condition that it shall not, by way of trade or otherwise, be lent, resold, hired out, or otherwise circulated, without the publisher's prior consent, in any form of binding or cover other than that in which it is published.

a tree of my Own

Ruskin Bond

Illustrated by

Barkha Lohia

talking CUB

An Imprint of Speaking Tiger Books

Eight years have passed
Since I placed my cherry seed in the grass.
'Must have a tree of my own,' I said—
And watered it once and went to bed

And forgot; but cherries have a way of growing
Though no one's caring very much or knowing,
And suddenly that summer, near the end of May,
I found a tree had come to stay.

It was very small,
a five months' child,
Lost in the tall grass running wild.
Goats ate the leaves,
a grasscutter's scythe
Split it apart, and a monsoon blight
Shrivelled the slender stem...Even so,
Next spring I watched three new shoots grow,

The young tree struggle, upwards thrust
Its arms in fresh fierce lust
For light and air and sun.
I could only wait, as one
Who watches, wondering, while Time and the rain
Made a miracle from green, growing pain...

I went away next year—
Spent a season in Kashmir—
Came back thinner, rather poor,
But richer by a cherry tree at my door.

Six feet high, my own dark cherry,
And—I could barely believe it—a berry,
Ripened and jewelled in the sun,
Hung from a branch—just one!

And next year there were
blossoms, small
Pink, fragile, quick to fall

At the merest breath, the sleepiest breeze...
I lay on the grass, at ease,
Looked up through the leaves, at the blue
Blind sky, at the finches as they flew
And flitted through the dappled green,

While bees in an ecstasy drank
Of nectar from each bloom, and the sun sank
Swiftly, and the stars turned in the sky,
And moon-moths and singing crickets and I—
Yes, I!—praised night and stars and tree:
A small, tall cherry grown by me.

RUSKIN BOND is the author of numerous novels, short-story collections and non-fiction books, many of them classics. Among them are *When I Was a Boy*, *Lone Fox Dancing*, *The Room on the Roof*, *A Flight of Pigeons*, and *A Book of Simple Living*. He received the Sahitya Akademi Award in 1993, the Padma Shri in 1999 and the Padma Bhushan in 2014.

BARKHA LOHIA is an illustrator based out of Gurugram. When she is not creating picture books and illustrating, she can be found wandering the jungle spaces in and around Delhi, photographing and sketching.